Wood-Fired Pizza Oven

Wood-Fired Pizza Oven

Make your own pizza oven
Create the perfect pizza

John Pellicano

NEW HOLLAND

DEDICATION
In memory of my father Fortunato Pellicano who passed away 30 years to the day he built our first wood-fired oven.

Contents

Introduction

I can still remember the day in 1979, when my father Fortunato ('Lucky') Pellicano built the first of our wood-fired ovens next to our shed in the suburb where I grew up. As a boy, I watched my father work on his prized pizza oven with some awe… the way he built the oven from scratch using simple, everyday materials. As a young man in the 1980s, I helped him build the last of three pizza ovens when we moved house; improving on our basic design and producing an oven that still stands and is in fine working order to this day.

I would like to share the secrets of building an outdoor wood-fired pizza oven with you. You may find it easier than you think, and the result will be hours of happy cooking for your family and friends. To help you along, I have included 40 of my favourite, easy to make pizza recipes, including my family recipe for pizza dough as well as a variety of pizza sauces which will be used as a base for a selection of toppings.

The number and variety of foods you can actually cook in an outdoor oven may surprise you … breads, roasts, chicken wings, beef ribs and vegetables of all kinds can all be cooked outdoors.

I have also added some maintenance tips to maximise your outdoor pizza oven experience!

Happy cooking!

Buon appetito e' mangiare bene
John Pellicano
May 2014

Building an outdoor wood-fired pizza oven

To construct your wood fire oven you will require the following materials, tools and equipment:
- Measuring tape, carpenter's pencil and ball of string
- 80 common bricks for the four pillars
- 4 stainless steel flat bars to support the oven on the pillars
- 1 tonne dry sand
- 1 ½ - 2 inch (35-50 mm) compressed fibre cement sheeting
- 64 smooth clay brick pavers
- 4 ½ inch stainless steel flue pipe (at least 50 cm long)
- 4 bags heat proof cement
- 150 fire resistant bricks
- 3 square metres of chicken wire
- sheet of plywood board
- large cardboard box (or sheets of heavy duty cardboard)

Tools
- spirit level
- measuring tape
- wheel barrel
- brick trowel
- rubber mallet
- bolster
- hammer
- diamond tipped saw (or equivalent) to cut through 4cm thick fibre cement sheeting

Note: If you buy the fibre cement sheet precut and measure the brick positions carefully before cementing, you shouldn't need to cut!

Utensils for cooking and maintenance
- Large pizza spatula for retrieving the pizza from the heart of the oven
- Large bowls
- Scraper
- Measuring cups
- Old straw broom (plastic will melt!)
- Shovel to remove ashes
- Old mop

STEP 1

- First, choose a nice position in your backyard that is covered from the sun and protected from rain to build your wood fire oven. Make sure the ground is firm and even so you can start building the four pillars.
- It is strongly recommended that three pillars are used on each side. Each pillars should be 1 ½ bricks wide with a distance of roughly two bricks in between each pillar. The distance between the front pillar and back pillar should be roughly 2m, to be able to support the 2m x 2m compressed fibre cement sheet. Please check that the sheet fits before cementing into place!
- It is also highly recommended that footings are dug and cement be placed to a depth of 60cm to support the structure.
- Before digging the footings, position the pillars, ensuring they are square to the other pillars, and place two bricks on the ground in between the pillars (1½ + 2 + 1 ½ +2 + 1½ = 8 ½ bricks). Remember to allow 2cm between bricks for the cement! Note: If the sizing of the pizza oven does not suit your needs, simply adjust your dimensions. You also have the option of bricking around the base of that the fibre cement sheeting will rest on if you have that expertise available.
- Build your pillars with mortar, using a spirit level to ensure they are square and level, rising to waist height which should be around 10 bricks high.
- Cut the flat steel bars to size and place them on top of the pillars so you can lay your compressed fibre cement sheet on top of it.
- Measure the dimensions between the pillars and cut the sheeting to fit. Ideally, the sheeting you place on top will square it all up!

STEP 2

- Around the edge of the compressed fibre cement sheet, build a retaining wall one brick high and allow the cement to dry overnight.

STEP 3

- Fill the top of the compressed fibre cement sheeting with dry compacted sand. The brick pavers will sit on top of it so make sure that you pour in and compact enough sand so that the pavers will finish flush with the top of retaining wall.

STEP 4

- Arrange smooth, clay brick pavers on the sand, softly tapping down with the rubber mallet so each clay brick paver is level and tightly compacted. Make sure there are no gaps or unlevelled pavers as the oven won't retain the heat and the pizza will get stuck in gaps!

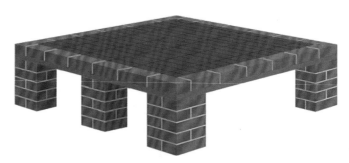

STEP 5

- Measure to find the centre of the oven table and draw a circle to give you a template for the external wall of the oven. This can be easily done by holding a round piece of dowel or curtain rod in the dead centre of the table and attaching a piece of string with a pencil at one end around the base of dowel.
- Simply pull the string tight to the edges of the bricks and trace the circle with the pencil while holding the centre rod firm.

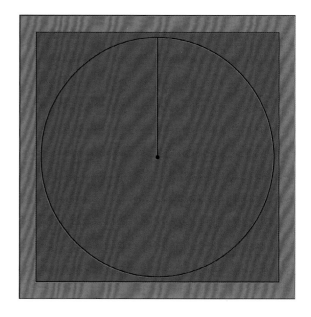

STEP 6

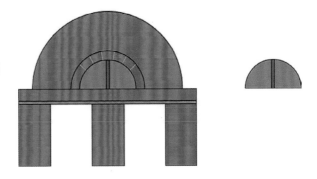

- The oven opening needs to be at least two-thirds of the height of the internal dome height and measure 60cm wide and 50cm high. If it is too high the heat will escape, and if the arch is too low the fire will not get enough oxygen to stay alight.
- Cut a semi-circle of plywood . 60cm x 50cm to use as the formwork for the row of bricks that go over the opening. The rows of bricks are positioned longways, facing into the centre of the oven. The height of this oven is 75cm.
- Cement a row of bricks over the plywood, remembering to angle the bricks inwards to make the arch shape.

STEP 7

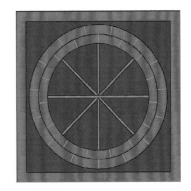

- Arrange full bricks inside the circle template that you have drawn, angling the corners of the bricks inward to keep the circular shape (the corners of the bricks facing inward should almost be touching each other). Once you have placed the bricks in the shape of the circle, go back and cement them into place, completing the circle and filling the gaps with mortar.

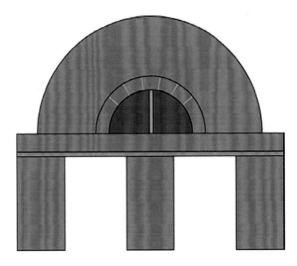

- Measure the distance across the inside of the oven, and using this as the diameter draw and cut four semi-circles using the cardboard box. These need to be cut in half again and each section (a quadrant) positioned inside the oven like the spokes of a while. They will act as both a guide and a support for each subsequent row of bricks, which will be laid on an angle to five it an 'igloo' shape. Don't worry about them becoming jammed inside the oven.

- On the second row of bricks, using full bricks again, add a little more mortar under the outside edge of the brick to give a slight tilt to the brickwork. Repeat with the third row of bricks. The oven's external wall should take on an 'igloo' shape. Don't worry if it looks a little untidy, the outside wall will later be rendered.
- Allow the mortar to dry overnight.
- In the remaining levels, use half bricks to help get the inward curve. Use a bolster and hammer to break the bricks – or the trowel if you don't have a bolster – by hitting firmly across the middle of the brick.
- Build your next three levels with half bricks, slowly making the tilt using a little more cement on outside. Allow to dry overnight.
- The final rows of the oven are very delicate so use the cardboard arches inside the oven as a guide and support.
- As you reach the fourth last row, position the stainless steel flue pipe at the front of the oven, cementing around it so as not to leave gaps.
- When you finish laying all the bricks, make sure you fill all the gaps with mortar and allow to dry for two days.

1st row is 36 round bricks, 11 bricks high

Full Brick, 3 rows up

Half Brick, 8 rows up

Flute

STEP 8
- Allow the oven to dry, place the chicken wire over the outside dome and cover it with a 1½ inch (38 mm) thick layer with the heat-proof mortar. Make it smooth and be sure there are no gaps anywhere. Clean off all excess mortar and allow a further three days to dry to avoid cracking when you light your first fire.
- Leave the cardboard arches inside the oven; they will be the first test at seeing if your oven has any air leaks. Set them alight and burn them, observing if the oven has a good flow of air during the fire.

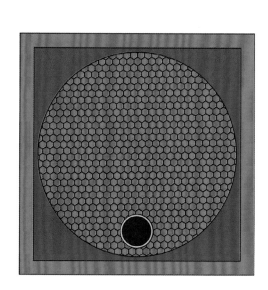

STEP 9

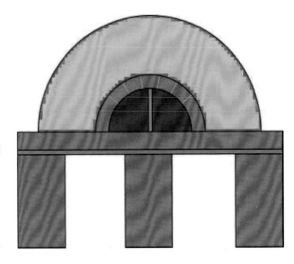

- Making your wood-fired oven hot enough to cook pizza is very important as you need not only the base of oven to be hot but the inner roof to retain heat. Start by filling your wood-fired oven with smaller pieces of wood to start you can also add charcoal to maintain a good heat. Once a fire has begun add large pieces
of wood (make sure all the wood is dry). It will take 35–50 minutes to get to a good heat going.
- As flames start to die down push the ashes to one corner of the oven using an old mop slightly making it damp clean floor of oven so you can have amber free pizza bases. To keep the oven at a constant heat, occasionally add a piece or two of wood.
- To see if wood-fired oven is hot enough to start cooking, throw a small amount of flour on the oven floor. If it turns golden brown slowly it means you're ready to start making pizza! If it burns straightaway, it's too hot. If it stays yellow, this means your oven is way too cool so add more wood.

Tips:
- Try not to cook pizzas if there are large flames … there should be a warm glow of heat.
- Always clean the oven after using, getting all ash out and clean the surface with an old broom and mop.
- Don't use treated wood or the chemicals will transfer into your food and you will be affected by the smoke.
- Also make sure you cover the front door so animals or drunk friend don't go in after using as the heat will be retained for a few hours.

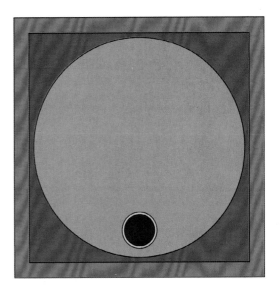

Ingredients

FLOUR

There are two main types of wheat grown today, hard and soft, each with a characteristic kernel composition and each with its own specific culinary use. The wheat kernel varies in 'hardness', which is the measure of protein content and consequently determines the flour's gluten content. Hard flour contains large protein chunks and relatively little starch. As a result this flour forms a strong gluten when mixed with water and is commonly used in bread making. In comparison soft flours contain a higher starch content and consequently develop a weaker gluten. Soft flours are more commonly used for pasta and cakes in which the texture is meant to be more tender and crumbly. Gluten stretches when worked and allows air to be incorporated and trapped, resulting in air bubbles in the dough. Bread making requires a hard flour in order for the carbon dioxide, released by the yeast, to be incorporated by the gluten, enabling the dough to rise. Pizza dough does not require the same level of rising action as a loaf of bread and many people claim that a softer flour is actually better. The following is a guide to the different flours available and their uses.

Semolina – a coarse grain produced from the hardest kind of wheat grown today. This is predominantly used for very stiff doughs, particularly dried pastas. It is too hard for bread- or pasta-making but can be added to pizza doughs for texture and crunch.

Hard flour (strong bread flour) – grade 1 contains the highest gluten level and is generally used for bread making or pizzas.

Soft flour (standard flour) – grade 00 (*doppio zero*) is the finest grade and contains less gluten. It is useful for pasta making and baking. Soft flour can be used for pizza making but make sure the packet states that it is 'panifiable', meaning that it is suitable for bread making.

YEAST

Yeasts are a group of single-celled funghi and about 160 different species are known. It is one species in particular, *Saccharomyces cerevisiae* or 'brewer's sugar fungus', that is good for brewing and baking. Yeast gives off a characteristic sour flavour and smell; it leavens bread (meaning it causes it to ferment and rise) and converts the grain carbohydrates into alcohol and carbon dioxide. When we buy fresh yeast it is live but inactive. With a little warmth and the addition of some water it is activated and releases the gas – carbon dioxide – that raises the dough. The activity ceases only when the dough is placed in the oven and the yeast is killed by extreme heat.

Fresh yeast – this should be putty-like in colour and texture; it should look firm and moist and feel cool to the touch. If it is dry, dark and crumbly it may be stale or not live. Fresh yeast can be bought for a pittance from many supermarkets that have a bakery on site or from a local bakery. Keep fresh yeast in an airtight container in the refrigerator for up to 3 days. Alternatively, divide the yeast into 15 g or 30 g (½ oz or 1 oz) portions and freeze it for up to 3 months. Always defrost the yeast thoroughly at room temperature or in the refrigerator before use.

To use: using a spoon, crumble the fresh yeast into a small glass bowl and add about a quarter of the required amount of water as specified in the recipe. Use the back of the spoon to cream the yeast until it dissolves in the water and forms a smooth blended paste. Stir in the remaining water. The yeast mixture is now ready to be added to the flour.

Dried granular yeast – usually bought in glass jars from the supermarket. Dried yeast can be reconstituted with a little lukewarm water and will give exactly the same result as fresh yeast. It must be stored in an airtight container. Always keep an eye on the date stamp. If it doesn't produce a frothy head when reconstituted with water it is not fresh.

To use: sprinkle dried granular yeast into a small glass bowl containing the quantity of lukewarm water specified in the recipe. Leave to dissolve for 5–10 minutes. Once the yeast has dissolved, stir the mixture with a wooden spoon. The yeast mixture is now ready to be added to the flour. Continue as instructed in the recipe.

Dried easy-blend yeast – the easiest of yeasts to use as it is just added to the flour, with the water added separately. Again, the end product will be just as superior as if it were made using fresh or granular yeast. Always check the date stamp to ensure freshness.

To use: sprinkle dried easy-blend yeast directly onto the flour. The yeast will activate once the liquid has been added. Continue as instructed in the recipe. Easy-blend yeast cannot be used for the 'sponge' method.

NOTES
- 15 g (½ oz) fresh yeast = 2 teaspoons dried granular yeast = 2 teaspoons dried powdered yeast
- In the recipes we have used dried granular yeast and the method has been written to reflect this. If you want to use other types of yeast when making the recipes, refer back to these pages.

PIZZA BASES

There is great satisfaction to be had in making your own pizza bases. Not only is the kneading process a great way to relieve tension in your body but the end result will also taste better than any bought alternative! It is important, when making bread, to understand your ingredients and what they do in order to achieve the best result possible. Environmental factors such as temperature and humidity will all play a part, as will the age of the flour you use, the hardness of the water you incorporate and the freshness of the yeast. One single bread-making experience will never be the same as the next. If the dough feels a little dry then add more liquid; if it is too wet then add a little more flour. With practice you will become familiar with how it should look and feel and will develop an instinct for adding a little more of one ingredient and a little less of another. As always, these recipes are guidelines to which you can adhere as much or as little as you like. If you are pressed for time, there are alternatives to making your own base which can make your pizza-making experience quick and easy and with a delicious end result.

PIZZA DOUGH MAKING

Mixing – this involves the mixing together of flour, water and yeast – as simple as that. Once mixed the gluten proteins begin to unfold and form water-protein complexes. Secondly, the yeast begins to feed on the sugars in the flour and starts the process of fermentation and the production of carbon dioxide. In some recipes we use a 'sponge' method, which involves mixing up to half of the flour in with the yeast and water mixture. This can give a slightly more aerated end product due to the longer time of fermentation.

Kneading – this improves the aeration of the dough and furthers the development of the gluten. It is best done by hand if you prefer a product with larger air bubbles, though some bread machines and food mixers do have dough hooks, which will create bread with a very fine, cake-like texture. Your technique for kneading will determine the final texture of your pizza base. Your dough is well kneaded when it takes on a silky, satiny appearance. Rich, buttery or sweet doughs generally require longer kneading than others.

Rising (fermentation) – the stage when the dough is set aside and covered with a clean tea (kitchen) towel in a warm place. The gluten development is still happening but the main activity is the multiplication of yeast cells, which causes the dough to rise and expand. The yeast is producing more carbon dioxide which, in turn, expands the air pockets resulting in the final bread texture. The dough should approximately double in size and then it is ready. At this stage it is important to knead (punch back) the dough to release the pressure, shape it and leave it for another short rising. Then it is ready to be rolled out and topped.

Baking – when the dough is initially put in the oven it will experience a sudden expansion as the heat will cause a rapid production of carbon dioxide. When the interior of the dough reaches about 60°C (140°F) the yeast cells will die and the rising will cease. The dough will then undergo a phase of browning that will give the dough its crispy texture. Perfectly cooked dough should sound hollow when tapped.

FREEZING DOUGH

Your dough can be frozen as dough balls after the rising (fermentation) stage. Just knock the dough back, reshape into a ball and place in a freezer bag. Remove the dough from the freezer about 6–8 hours before you need it. Leave it to defrost at room temperature. When you are ready, turn the plastic bag inside out and, using a floured hand, pull the dough from the bag. Knead the dough on a lightly floured surface for 5 minutes. Shape into a ball and leave for 20 minutes before rolling it out.

PIZZA BASE ALTERNATIVES

Pitta bread – use pitta breads to make mini or individual pizzas, which are great for the kids. Let them top their own and experiment with the ingredients.

Tortillas – these make a thin and crispy base. These can also be cooked in a frying pan and even topped with a second tortilla to make a quesadilla. Great served as a quick finger-food snack chopped into wedges.

Naan bread – choose an Indian-inspired topping, such as spinach and paneer cheese, and finish it off with an authentic naan bread base. This is a breadier alternative to tortillas.

Puff pastry – it's hard to say whether making a pizza with puff pastry is cheating or not. Most of us would call this a tart but it's basically the same concept and a quick and easy alternative if you buy ready-rolled sheets.

Bought bases – bought pizza bases come in many shapes and forms and are available from all good supermarkets. Try frozen, vacuum-packed or ready-rolled bases from the chiller cabinet. Some supermarkets or delicatessens may sell frozen balls of pizza dough, which just require defrosting, and shaping. Alternatively, your local Italian restaurant may sell you frozen balls of dough.

OLIVE OIL

We've used extra virgin olive oil in our recipes. Olive oils vary considerably in taste and strength. Choose one with a flavour you like. In some cases we use infused olive oils, such as chilli or basil oil.

Infused oils – you can buy these or make your own. To infuse oils, firstly wash and dry your chosen herb or spice and lightly bruise it (put pressure on it) to release the flavour. Place the herbs or spices in a clean, sterilized jar or bottle and cover with warmed oil. Seal tightly and leave in a cool, dark place to infuse for about 2 weeks. Leave the herbs and spices in if you want a stronger flavour or a decorative look, otherwise strain. Use the oils within 2 months of initial bottling. Some suggested flavourings are basil, chilli, rosemary, thyme, tarragon, cardamom, star anise or cloves.

TOMATOES

There are more than 5,000 varieties of tomato in the world today varying from yellow cherry tomatoes and green plum tomatoes to red beef tomatoes. Tomatoes transform white pizza bread into a rich and flavourful meal. Italian cooking without tomatoes would truly be unthinkable. Tomatoes can be bought in many varieties: fresh, canned, puréed, sun-dried and semi-dried are all readily available today. Tomatoes are made up of about 94 per cent water and must always be well drained, whether fresh or canned, in order to avoid a soggy pizza.

Canned tomatoes – these are scalded, peeled and slightly salted before being canned. Canned tomatoes are a very popular choice for pizza makers today and are of equal quality to the fresh variety. In many cases it is the superior, unblemished tomatoes that are sent away for canning when the not so perfect tomatoes are left behind for fresh sale.

Tomato purée – many professional pizza makers steer clear of tomato purée, arguing that it tends to dull the other flavours, making all pizzas taste the same. We're not sure if this is truly the case and it is certainly a useful ingredient if you want to assemble a pizza in a hurry.

Preparing tomatoes

When you select fresh tomatoes for topping a pizza or making pizza sauce, choose varieties that have a high proportion of flesh to seeds and juice; these are often labelled as plum, pear or paste tomatoes. Select tomatoes that are fragrant and fully ripe and keep them out of the refrigerator if you want to maintain peak flavour.

- Use a paring knife to core the tomatoes. Turn the tomatoes over and slit the skin in an X-shaped cut.
- Put the tomatoes in a pan containing enough boiling water to cover them and boil for 15 seconds.
- Remove them with a slotted spoon and put them in a bowl of cold water. Leave for a few seconds.
- Remove them from the cold water and use a paring knife to pull off the skins.
- Halve the tomatoes horizontally with a chopping knife. Hold each half over a bowl, cut side down, and squeeze to remove the seeds.
- Chop the tomatoes into small pieces.

CHEESES

Mozzarella – *mozzarella di bufala* is the original mozzarella and is delicious served as is. It is sweet in flavour and soft in texture but does not melt as well as cow's mozzarella. Cow's milk mozzarella is the one to use for cooking. It has a very mild, creamy and faintly sour flavour and melts beautifully, making it ideal for pizzas. Mozzarella can also be made with goats' milk, which is a little sharper in taste and is not such a popular choice.

Mozzarella is produced as a semi-soft, fresh cheese or a firm block of cheese made with low-or non-fat milk. The fresh cheese is the ultimate choice for home-made pizzas but it is important to make sure you drain and dry it well to remove as much excess moisture as possible. Fresh mozzarella balls are usually packaged in water or, brine or whey, to preserve freshness. Fresh mozzarella is mild in flavour, soft and very pliable. The longer that mozzarella ages the softer and sourer it becomes. In all our recipes we have used fresh mozzarella unless otherwise specified.

Mozzarella can also be found in other forms:
- Block mozzarella – block mozzarella is lower in moisture than fresh mozzarella and is often the preferred choice for many commercial pizza makers. In America as many as 90 per cent of all commercial pizza makers will use block mozzarella. It is lower in fat and consequently not as flavoursome as fresh mozzarella. Bocconcini – small mozzarella balls usually about 1 in (2.5 cm) in diameter.

- wood chips and is darker in colour than standard mozzarella.
- Mozzarella scamorza – this mozzarella has been heavily smoked, usually over pecan shells, and is much darker in colour and denser in texture.
- Mozzarella pearls – tiny balls of mozzarella, which are about 1.5 cm (⅝ in) in diameter. They are available from some supermarkets but if you can't find them then a large mozzarella ball cut into cubes is exactly the same.

Mozzarella can be wrapped in plastic food wrap (cling film) and frozen for up to 3 months. Frozen mozzarella does decrease in flavour and may become moister in texture. Before serving or cooking allow the cheese to defrost in the refrigerator before removing and warming to room temperature. Fresh mozzarella usually keeps for up to 2 weeks when chilled.

Parmesan

When buying Parmesan always look for the words *Parmigiano reggiano* for authenticity and quality. Never buy pre-grated (shredded) or shaved Parmesan in tubs. It is important to keep Parmesan from drying out so always buy a freshly cut piece and grate (shred) it only when needed. Parmesan cheese is rich and round in flavour and has the ability to melt with heat and become inseparable from the ingredients to which it is added. To store Parmesan for longer than 2–3 weeks divide it into pieces, each with a piece of rind still attached, and wrap tightly in greaseproof paper (baking paper), then in heavy duty aluminium foil. Store on the bottom shelf of the refrigerator.

Pecorino

The Italian word for sheep is *pecora*, hence all cheese made from sheep's milk is called pecorino. There are dozens of pecorinos available: some are soft and fresh while others are crumbly and sharp, more like a Parmesan.

Fontina

Fontina is a semi-hard cheese with a creamy texture and subtle nutty flavour. It is a very useful cheese for cooking as it has good melting properties, making it a popular choice in fondues and pizzas. Fontina is made from unpasteurized cow's milk from the grazing cows of the Val d'Aosta alpine region of Italy.

Ricotta

The word *ricotta* literally means 'recooked' in Italian. It is made from the whey of other cheeses that is cooked again to make a milky white, soft, granular and mild tasting cheese. Ricotta does not melt.

Gruyère

Gruyère is a firm cheese with a nutty flavour. For culinary purposes it is best when finely grated (shredded).

Asiago

A semi-firm to hard Italian cheese with a nutty, sharp flavour that is mainly used for grating (shredding). Asiago was traditionally made with sheep's milk, but it is now more commonly made with cow's milk.

Monterey Jack
Monterey Jack is a Cheddar-style cheese first made in California using pasteurized cow's milk. It is commonly sold by itself, or mixed with Colby cheese to make a marbled cheese known as Colby-Jack (or Co-Jack).

Cheddar
Choose a mature Cheddar for the best flavour and always grate (shred) for use on pizza to get a more even melt.

Provolone
This is a southern Italian cheese that is pale yellow in colour, with a smooth texture. Milder, fresh provolone can be eaten on its own, although once aged it is generally used in cooking.

Gorgonzola
Gorgonzola is a mild and creamy blue-veined cheese. Choose dolcelatte if you prefer a creamier, milder soft blue cheese.

Taleggio
Taleggio is a semi-soft cheese made from whole cow's milk. Its flavour can range from mild to pungent, depending on its age. When young, the colour of taleggio is pale yellow. As it ages it darkens to deep yellow and becomes rather runny. Taleggio is sold in blocks and is covered either with a wax coating or a thin mould.

Mascarpone
Mascarpone is a soft, unripened cheese that belongs to the cream cheese family. It comes from northern Italy and is a thick, rich, sweet and velvety, ivory-coloured cheese produced from cow's milk that has the texture of sour cream. It is sold in plastic tubs and can be found in most delicatessens and good supermarkets.

CURED MEATS

Prosciutto

Prosciutto is the pig's hind thigh or ham that has been salted and air-dried. The salt draws off the meat's excess water, thus curing and preserving it. A true prosciutto is never smoked. When served it should always be thinly sliced and used as soon as possible. If you are not consuming it immediately then each slice or each single layer of slices must be covered with greaseproof (baking) paper or plastic wrap (cling film) then wrapped in aluminium foil. Prosciutto is delicious eaten as it is or cooked on pizzas. It can be quite salty so do not add extra salt unless needed.

Pancetta

Pancetta is from the pig's belly and is the Italian equivalent of bacon. Pancetta can be bought sliced or cubed and is more tender and considerably less salty than prosciutto. It can also be eaten raw or cooked. Pancetta is rarely ever smoked except in a few areas of northern Italy.

Salami

Salami is the generic term for cured and fermented meat (usually pork or beef) that is typically flavoured with spices such as black pepper, fennel, chilli or paprika. The meat mixture is ground and stuffed into casings then hung to dry, either in hot or cool air, until the sausages have reduced in weight by at least half. Some salamis or cured sausages will additionally be smoked. Examples of common salamis and cured sausages are Napoli, Milano, Genoa, chorizo and pepperoni.

DOUGH

BASIC PIZZA DOUGH

3 teaspoons dry instant yeast
1¼ pints (3 cups/750 ml) warm
 water
6 tablespoons olive oil, plus extra for
 greasing
2 oz (½ cup/60 g) wholemeal (whole-
 wheat) flour

2 teaspoons salt
1 lb 6 oz (5½ cups/600 g) plain
 (all-purpose) flour, plus extra for
 dusting

Put the yeast in a large bowl, add the warm water and leave for 10 minutes until it dissolves and becomes creamy.

Stir in the olive oil, wholemeal flour, salt and plain flour into the yeast mixture. Mix well until combined.

Tip the dough out onto a lightly floured surface and knead until smooth and elastic.

Lightly rub the dough surface with olive oil and place in a clean bowl. Cover with damp cloth and set aside in a warm place to double in volume, about 45 minutes.

Turn the dough out onto a lightly floured surface and knead again (punch down). Divide into 3 equal rounds and rest for another 3 minutes.

Roll out each with a rolling pin, or use your hands, into a 12 in (30 cm) round.

NOTE: Make sure when you're mixing the flour into the yeast mixture that there are no flour pockets (that is flour that didn't mix through).

PIZZA DOUGH

¼ oz (7 g) sachet active dry yeast
1 pint (2½ cups/600 ml) warm
    water
2 tablespoons olive oil, plus extra for
    greasing
2 oz (½ cup/60 g) wholemeal
    (whole-wheat) flour
1 tablespoon salt
1 lb 6 oz (5½ cups/600 g) bread

flour, plus extra for dusting
1 teaspoon granulated sugar

MAKES 3 PIZZA BASES

Put the yeast in a large bowl, add the warm water and leave for 10 minutes until its dissolves and becomes creamy.

Stir in the olive oil, wholemeal flour, salt, sugar and 4 cups (1 lb 2 oz/500 g) of the bread flour. Mix well, then slowly add the remaining bread flour a little at a time until fully incorporated.

Tip out the dough onto a lightly floured surface and knead until smooth and elastic.

Lightly rub the surface of the dough with olive oil, then return it to a clean bowl, cover with a damp cloth and set aside in warm place to double in volume, about 1 hour.

Tip out the dough onto a lightly floured surface, and knead lightly (punch down). Divide the dough into 3 equal rounds and set aside to rest for another 10 minutes.

Roll out each round, using a rolling pin or your hands, to a 12 in (30 cm) round.

NOTE: Elastic means that you can stretch the dough without it ripping.

FOOD PROCESSOR PIZZA DOUGH

10 oz (2½ cups/275 g) plain (all-purpose) flour, plus extra for dusting
¼ oz (7 g) fast-rising active dry yeast
¼ teaspoon salt
8 fl oz (1 cup/250 ml) very warm water (about 122°F/50°C)
1 teaspoon honey

2 teaspoons olive oil, plus extra for greasing

MAKES 1 PIZZA BASE

In the bowl of a food processor fitted with a steel blade, mix the flour, yeast and salt. Combine the water, honey and olive oil in a measuring cup. With the processor running, pour the water mixture through the feed tube in a steady stream, adjusting the amount poured so the flour can absorb it. Turn the processor off when the dough gathers into clumps and before it forms a smooth ball. Do not over process – it should feel sticky. If it is too soft, add more flour, 1 tablespoon at a time, until the dough has a firm consistency.

Knead by processing for an additional 45 seconds or knead by hand until the dough is smooth and silky. Shape into a ball.

Place the dough in an oiled bowl and turn to coat evenly. Cover with plastic wrap (cling film) and leave to rise in a warm place until doubled in size, 30–40 minutes.

Tip the dough out onto a lightly floured surface and knead (punch down) the dough. Cover with the inverted bowl, and set aside to rest for 10 minutes.

On a lightly floured surface, roll out the dough to the desired size. Any excess dough can be wrapped in cling film and refrigerated.

NOTE: A food processor fitted with a steel blade can mix pizza dough in seconds. If your food processor is powerful enough to handle heavy yeast doughs without damaging the motor, you can also use it to knead the dough. If necessary, mix the ingredients in the food processor and complete the kneading by hand.

CHEESE PIZZA DOUGH

1½ teaspoons dry yeast
1½ tablespoons olive oil
½ teaspoon sugar
10 oz (275 g/2½ cups) plain
  (all-purpose) flour
2 oz (55 g) mature Cheddar cheese,
  grated (shredded)
1 teaspoon salt

MAKES 1 PIZZA BASE

Place the yeast, oil, sugar and ¼ pint (150 ml/⅔ cup) warm water in a large bowl and mix to dissolve. Set aside in a warm, draught-free place for 5 minutes or until foamy.

Put the flour, cheese and salt in a food processor and pulse once or twice to mix. With the machine running, slowly pour in the oil and yeast mixture and process to form a rough dough. Turn the dough out onto a lightly floured surface and knead for 5 minutes or until soft and shiny. Add more flour, if necessary.

Lightly oil a large bowl, then roll the dough around in it to cover the surface with oil. Cover tightly with cling wrap (cling film) and place in a warm, draught-free place for 1½–2 hours or until doubled in volume. Punch down and remove the dough from the bowl. Knead briefly before using as desired.

GLUTEN-FREE PIZZA DOUGH

2 teaspoons dry yeast
12 fl oz (1½ cups/375 ml) warm
    water
15 oz (3¾ cups/425 g) gluten-free
    plain (all-purpose) flour, plus extra
    for dusting

1 teaspoon salt
3 tablespoons olive oil, 1 to rub on
    the dough so it does not dry out.

MAKES 3 PIZZA BASES

Pour the yeast into a large bowl, add the warm water and set aside for 10 minutes until the yeast dissolves and becomes creamy.

Stir the flour and salt into the yeast mixture and mix well until the dough comes together. Tip the dough out onto a lightly floured surface and knead until smooth and elastic.

Lightly rub the dough ball with 1 tablespoon of the oil and return it to the bowl. Cover with a damp cloth and set aside in a warm place until doubled in volume, about 50 minutes.

Tip the dough out onto a lightly floured surface again and knead (punch down) lightly. Divide into 3 equal rounds and set aside to rest for another 5 minutes.

Roll out each dough ball on a lightly floured surface to a 12 in (30 cm) round using a rolling pin or your hands.

MAMMA'S PIZZA DOUGH

1¾ oz (50 g) fresh yeast
435 fl oz (1¾ cups) warm water
1 lb 2 oz (500 g/4½ cups) strong
  white bread flour, plus extra for
  dusting
3 teaspoons salt
3 tablespoons olive oil, plus extra for
  greasing

In large bowl dissolve the yeast in the warm water. Set aside for 10 minutes until its dissolves and becomes creamy.

Sift the flour and salt into a clean bowl and make a well in the centre. Pour in the yeast mixture and mix well.

Slowly add the olive oil. When dough comes together, tip it out onto a lightly floured surface and knead until smooth and elastic.

Lightly rub the dough ball with oil and return it to the cleaned bowl. Cover with damp cloth and set aside in a warm place until doubled in volume, about 45 minutes.

Tip the dough out again onto a lightly floured surface and knead (punch back) lightly . Divide the dough into 3 equal rounds and set aside to rest for another 5 minutes.

Roll out each ball on a lightly floured surface, using a rolling pin or your hands, to a 12 in (30 cm) round.

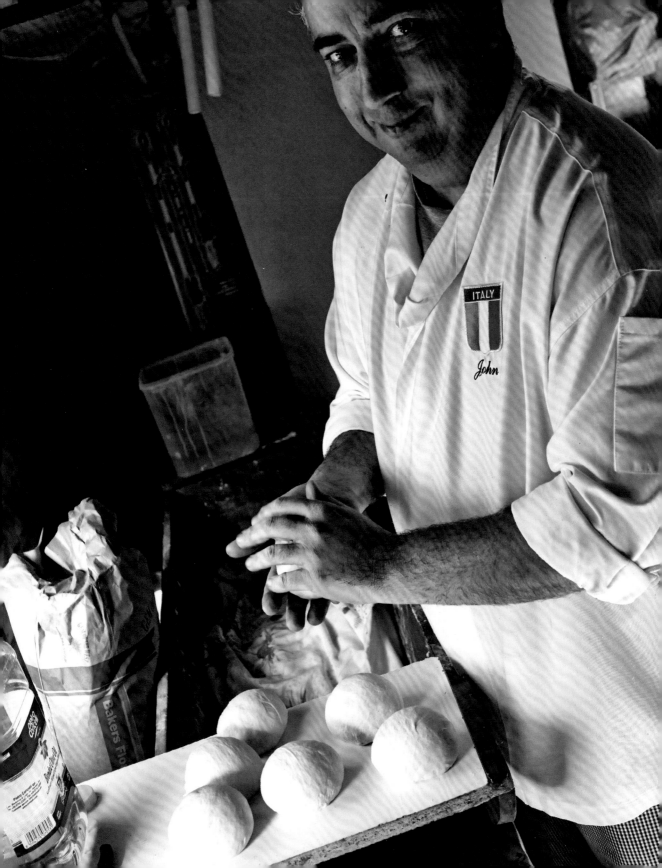

HERB PIZZA DOUGH

1½ teaspoons dry yeast
½ teaspoon sugar
1½ tablespoons olive oil, plus extra
   for greasing
¼ pint (⅔ cup/150 ml) warm water
1 teaspoon dried mixed herbs

10 oz (275 g/2½ cups) plain
   (all-purpose) flour, plus extra for
   dusting
1 teaspoon salt

MAKES 1 PIZZA BASE

Put the yeast, sugar, oil and ¼ pint (150 ml/⅔ cup) warm water in a large bowl and mix to dissolve. Set aside in a warm, draught-free place for 5 minutes or until foamy.

Put the flour, herbs and salt in a food processor and pulse once or twice to sift. With the machine running, slowly pour in the oil and yeast mixture and process to form a rough dough. Turn the dough onto a lightly floured surface and knead for 5 minutes, or until soft and shiny. Add more flour, if necessary.

Lightly oil a large bowl, then roll the dough around in it to coat the surface. Cover the bowl tightly with cling film (plastic wrap) and place in a warm, draught-free place for 1½–2 hours, or until the dough has doubled in volume. Knock down and remove the dough from bowl. Knead briefly then roll out on a lightly floured surface to a 12 in (30 cm round).

TOMATO PIZZA DOUGH

1½ teaspoons dry yeast
½ teaspoon sugar
¼ pint (150 ml/⅔ cup) tomato juice,
  warmed
10 oz (2½ cups/275 g) plain (all-
  purpose) flour, plus extra for
  dusting
1 teaspoon salt

1½ tablespoons olive oil, plus extra
  for greasing

MAKES 1 PIZZA BASE

Place the yeast, sugar and tomato juice in a large bowl and mix to dissolve. Set aside in a warm, draught-free place for 5 minutes or until foamy.

Put the flour and salt in a food processor and pulse once or twice to mix. With the machine running, slowly pour in the oil and yeast mixture and process to form a rough dough. Turn the dough onto a lightly floured surface and knead for 5 minutes or until soft and shiny. Add more flour, if necessary.

Lightly oil a large bowl, then roll the dough around in it to coat the surface with oil. Cover tightly with cling film (plastic wrap) and place in a warm, draught-free place for 1½–2 hours, or until dough has doubled in volume. Knock down and remove the dough from the bowl. Knead briefly rolling out on a lightly floured surface to a 12 in (30 cm) round.

QUICK PIZZA DOUGH

¾ oz (21 g) dry yeast
6 teaspoons sugar
1½ pints (3¾ cups/900 ml) warm
 water
1 lb 14 oz (7½ cups/840 g) strong
 white bread flour, plus extra for
 dusting

2 teaspoons salt
3 tablespoons olive oil (1 to rub over
 the dough so it does not dry out)
 plus extra for greasing,

MAKES 3 PIZZA BASES

In large bowl dissolve the yeast and sugar in the warm water. Set aside for 15 minutes until its dissolves and becomes creamy.

Stir in the flour and salt and 2 tablespoons of oil and mix well. When dough comes together, turn out onto a lightly floured surface and knead until smooth and elastic.

Lightly rub the dough ball with 1 tablespoon of oil, return it to a clean bowl, cover with damp cloth and set aside in a warm place to double in volume, about 30 minutes.

Tip the dough out onto a lightly floured surface and knead (punch down) lightly then divide into 3 equal rounds and set aside to rest for another 5 minutes.

On a lightly floured surface, roll out each ball with a rolling pin or your hands to a 12 in (30 cm) round.

SINOPOLI PIZZA DOUGH

3 teaspoons dry instant yeast
16 fl oz (2 cups/500 ml) warm water
6 tablespoons olive oil, plus extra for
*   greasing 14 oz (3½ cups/400 g)*
*   strong white bread flour, plus extra*
*   for dusting*
2 teaspoons salt

MAKES 3 PIZZA BASES

In large bowl dissolve the yeast in the warm water and set aside for 10 minutes until it dissolves and becomes creamy.

Stir in the olive oil, flour and salt and mix well. When dough comes together, turn out onto a lightly floured surface and knead until smooth and elastic.

Lightly rub the dough ball with oil, then return it to a clean bowl, cover with a damp cloth and set aside in a warm place to double in volume, about 45 minutes.

Tip the dough out onto a floured surface, knead (punch down) lightly, then divide into 3 equal rounds and set aside to rest for another 3 minutes.

On a lightly floured surface, roll out each ball with a rolling pin or your hands to a 12 in (30 cm) round.

SAUCE

NAPOLITANA SAUCE

4½ lb (2 kg) ripe Roma tomatoes
2 large onions, diced
7 fl oz (200 ml) tomato paste
2 teaspoons dried oregano
Salt and pepper
½ cup fresh basil, torn
2 tablespoons olive oil

TOPS 5 PIZZAS

Remove the core from each tomato and then cut a cross in the opposite end. Blanch each tomato in a bowl of boiling water for 30 seconds, remove with a slotted spoon and place directly into cold water. Peel off the skin. Cut each into quarters and remove all the seeds.

In a saucepan, fry the onions in 2 tablespoons of oil until soft and transparent. Add the tomatoes and tomato paste and bring to the boil. Lower the heat and simmer gently for 45 minutes, breaking up the tomatoes when they soften. Add the dried oregano and seasoning, then the basil. Set aside to cool down.

SPICY SAUCE

4½ lb (2 kg) ripe Roma tomatoes
2 large onions, diced
6 fresh chillies, diced
2 red capsicum (bell peppers), diced
7 fl oz (200 ml) tomato paste
2 teaspoons dried oregano
½ cup fresh basil, torn
salt and pepper
2 tablespoon olive oil

TOPS 5 PIZZAS

Remove the core from each tomato and then cut a cross in the opposite end. Blanch each tomato in a bowl of boiling water for 30 seconds, remove with a slotted spoon and place directly into cold water. Peel off the skin. Cut each into quarters and remove all the seeds.

In a saucepan fry the onions in the oil until soft and transparent. Add the es, capsicum and prepared tomatoes. Mix to combine then add the tomato paste and bring to the boil. Lower the heat and simmer for 45 minutes. Once the tomatoes are soft mix around to break them up and add the dried oregano and seasoning.

Add the basil and allow to cool.

BOLOGNESE SAUCE

4½ lb (2 kg) ripe Roma tomatoes
2 large onions, diced
2¼ lb (1 kg) minced (ground) veal
7 fl oz (200 ml) tomato paste
2 teaspoons dried oregano
Salt and pepper
½ cup fresh basil, torn
2 tablespoon olive oil

Remove the core from each tomato and then cut a cross in the opposite end. Blanch each tomato in a bowl of boiling water for 30 seconds, remove with a slotted spoon and place directly into cold water. Peel off the skin. Cut each into quarters and remove all the seeds.

In a saucepan, fry the onions in oil until soft and transparent. Add the minced meat and fry until browned. Add the prepared tomatoes and mix in the tomato paste. Bring to the boil, lower the heat and simmer gently for 45 minutes. Once the tomatoes are soft, mix to break them up, add the oregano and seasoning.

Add the basil, stir to combine, then set aside to cool.

PESTO SAUCE

2 Bch (17½ oz/500 g) fresh basil,
  picked leaves
 6 garlic cloves
1 oz (¼ cup/30 g) pine nuts, roasted
4 oz (½ cup/115 g) Parmesan, grated
  (shredded)
2 fl oz (¼ cup/60 ml) olive oil

salt and pepper

TOPS 5 PIZZAS

Put the basil, garlic, pine nuts, Parmesan and olive oil in the bowl of a blender. Purée until smooth.

Season to taste with salt and pepper.

GARLIC OIL

15 garlic cloves
8 fl oz (1 cup/250 ml) olive oil
salt and pepper

Peel the garlic and put in the bowl of a blenderr with the olive oil. Purée until smooth.

Season with salt and pepper.

Store in an airtight glass and refrigerate until ready to use.

BARBEQUE SAUCE

1¾ pints (1 litre) barbeque sauce
2 fl oz (¼ cup/60 ml) Worcestershire
  sauce
2 teaspoons balsamic vinegar
Salt and pepper

TOPS 5 PIZZAS

Place all ingredients into a jar.

Place all the ingredients into a glass jar and shake well to infuse the flavours. Taste and season as required.

Store in an airtight glass container in the refrigerator.

SATAY SAUCE

½ cup smooth peanut butter
1 tsp garlic
¼ cup coconut cream

Blend all ingredients to a smooth paste

TOPS 1 PIZZA

MIXED HERB OIL

15 garlic cloves
¼ cup thyme, dried
¼ cup rosemary, dried
¼ cup marjoram, dried
¼ cup basil, dried
¼ cup oregano, dried
¼ cup Sage, dried
1¾ pints (1 litre) olive oil
salt and pepper

TOPS 5 PIZZAS

Place all the dried herbs into glass jar with the olive oil. Seal. Leave for 2 days to infuse the oil with the herb flavours.

Season to taste. Store in the airtight container in the refrigerator.

TANDOORI PASTE

1 tsp salt
1 tsp cayenne pepper
1 tsp coriander (cilantro) ground
1 tsp chilli powder
1 tsp garlic powder
1 tsp dry mustard powder
1 tsp ginger powder
1 tsp turmeric
1 tsp fennel seed
1 tsp cumin powder
1 tsp paprika
½ cup yogurt
2 tbsps lime juice

Blend all ingredients to a smooth paste

TOPS 1 PIZZA

PERI PERI MARINADE

10 medium sized chillis
pinch salt & pepper
½ lemon, juiced
2⅓ fl oz (100 ml/ ⅓ cup) olive oil
2 tbsp garlic powder

Blend all ingredients to a runny paste

TOPS 1 PIZZA

SALSA SAUCE

2 ripe tomatoes
½ red onion finely chopped
1 garlic clove crushed
2 tbsps limejuice
1 chilli, finely chopped
pinch salt & pepper

Combine all ingredients

TOPS 1 PIZZA

GUACAMOLE

1 ripe avocado
⅓ oz (10 g) finely chopped red onion
1 crushed garlic clove
2 tbsp lime juice
pinch salt & pepper

Mix all ingredients except red onion into a smooth paste then add onion.

TOPS 1 PIZZA

PIZZA

GARLIC PIZZA

1 pizza base
6 garlic cloves
2 fl oz (¼ cup/60 ml) olive oil
salt and pepper
1 handful fresh parsley, chopped, to
*   garnish*

MAKES 1 PIZZA

Put the garlic, olive oil and salt and pepper in a blender and blend to a pureé. Drizzle the purée evenly over the pizza base.

Put the pizza straight onto the pavers in the preheated wood-fired oven using the paddle.

Allow to cook for 10 minutes, rotating occasionally, until the base is golden brown.

Sprinkle with chopped parsley. Cut and serve.

MARGHERITA

1 pizza base
8 fl oz (1 cup/250 ml) Napolitana
   sauce (see recipe p. 53)
1 lb (2 cups/450 g) mozzarella cheese

1 handful fresh basil leaves, left
   whole (garnish)

MAKES 1 PIZZA

Spread Napolitana sauce evenly over the pizza base and top with mozzarella cheese.

Put the pizza straight onto the pavers in the preheated wood-fired oven using the paddle.

Allow to cook for 10 minutes, rotating occasionally until the base is golden brown and the cheese has melted.

Sprinkle with fresh basil leaves. Cut and serve.

NOTE: Don't overload the pizza with cheese or it won't melt properly.

BOCCONCINI

1 pizza base
8 fl oz (1 cup/250 ml) Napolitana
  sauce (see recipe p. 53)
1 lb (450 g/2 cups) Bocconcini
  cheese, sliced
Handful fresh basil leaves, to garnish

Spread Napolitana sauce evenly over the base and top with sliced bocconcini cheese.

Put the pizza straight onto pavers in the preheated wood-fired oven using the paddle.

Allow to cook for 10 minutes, rotating occasionally, until the base is golden brown and cheese has melted.

Scatter with fresh basil leaves. Cut and serve.

NOTE: Replace Napolitana sauce with thinly sliced tomato, if you like.

FOUR CHEESES

1 pizza base
8 fl oz (1 cup/250 ml) Napolitana
   sauce (see recipe p. 53)
2 oz (½ cup/60 g) mozzarella cheese
2 oz (½ cup/60 g) blue vein cheese
2 oz (½ cup/60 g) bocconcini cheese
2 oz (½ cup/60 g) feta cheese

rocket (arugula) to serve

MAKES 1 PIZZA

Spread Napolitana sauce evenly over the pizza base, top with the cheeses

Put the pizza straight onto the pavers in the preheated wood-fired oven using the paddle.

Allow to cook for 10 minutes, rotating occasionally, until the base is golden brown and the cheese has melted.

Arrange the rocket on top. Cut and serve.

NOTE: If you don't like any of these cheeses put your own favourites e.g., Camembert, tasty, provolone, parmesan. You can also make this with the Napolitana base.

FIG & GOATS' CHEESE

12 dried figs, quartered
1 pizza base
4 fl oz (½ cup/125 ml) olive oil
1 lb (450 g/2 cups) goats' cheese

MAKES 1 PIZZA

Put the figs in a bowl and pour over boiling water to cover. Set aside for 10 minutes while the figs soften.

Drizzle olive oil evenly over the pizza base then arrange the fig quarters over the top.

Put the pizza straight onto the pavers in the preheated wood-fired oven using the paddle.

Allow to cook for 10 minutes, rotating occasionally, until the base is golden brown.

Sprinkle with crumbled goats' cheese. Cut and serve.

MEDITERRANEAN

1 pizza base
6 oz (1 cup/180 g) Roma tomatoes
5 oz (1 cup/150 g) capsicum (bell
   pepper), strips
8 fl oz (1 cup/250 ml) Napolitana
   sauce (see recipe p. 53)
1½ oz (¼ cup/40 g) kalamata olives
1 lb (2 cups/450 g) feta cheese
2½ oz (½ cup/75 g) baby spinach
salt and pepper

MAKES 1 PIZZA

Quarter the tomatoes and arrange them in a baking tray with the capsicum. Roast for 10 minutes in the preheated wood-fired oven.

Spread the Napolitana sauce over the pizza base. Cover with roasted tomato, capsicum and olives.

Put the pizza straight onto the pavers in the preheated wood-fired oven using the paddle.

Allow to cook for 3–7 minutes, rotating occasionally, then remove from oven. Crumble the feta and baby spinach on top. Return to the oven for another 5 minutes, rotating until the base is golden brown. Season to taste.

Cut and serve.

NOTE: Crumble with goats' cheese or a creamier texture.

MEXICANA

1 pizza base
8 fl oz (1 cup/250 ml) Napolitana
  sauce (see recipe p. 53)
2½ oz (½ cup/75 g) red capsicum
  (bell pepper), diced
2½ oz (½ cup/75 g) green capsicum
  (bell pepper), diced
3 oz (½ cup/85 g) Spanish

(Bermuda) onion, diced
7 oz (200 g) cherry tomatoes, halved
1 ½ oz (½ cup/45 g) jalapeño
  peppers, sliced
1 lb (2 cups/450 g) mozzarella cheese

MAKES 1 PIZZA

Spread Napolitana sauce evenly over the pizza base. Arrange diced red and green capsicum, diced onion, cherry tomato halves and jalapeno peppers on top, then top with mozzarella cheese.

Put the pizza straight onto the pavers in the preheated wood-fired oven using the paddle.

Allow to cook for 10 minutes, rotating occasionally, until the base is golden brown and the cheese has melted.

Cut and serve.

MUSHROOM

1 pizza base
8 fl oz (1 cup/250 ml) Napolitana
  sauce (see recipe p. 53)
1 lb (2 cups/450 g) mozzarella cheese
½ cup onion, sliced
2 ½ oz (1 cup/75 g) mushrooms,
  sliced
1½ oz (¼ cup/40 g) kalamata olives

rocket (arugula), to serve

MAKES 1 PIZZA

Spread Napolitana sauce evenly over the pizza base. Arrange the sliced mushrooms, onions and olives on top, then sprinkle over mozzarella cheese.

Put the pizza straight onto the pavers in the preheated wood-fired oven using the paddle.

Allow to cook for 10 minutes, rotating occasionally, until the base is golden brown and the cheese has melted.

Place rocket on top, cut and serve

NOTE: Top with buffalo mozzarella instead of mozzarella.

MIXED HERB PIZZA

1 pizza base
2 fl oz (¼ cup/60 ml) olive oil
1 tablespoon dried rosemary
1 tablespoon dried oregano
1 tablespoon dried thyme
1 tablespoon dried basil
1 tablespoon dried marjoram
1 tablespoon dried sage
Salt and pepper

MAKES 1 PIZZA

Place all the dried herbs, olive oil and seasoning in a bowl. Cover and leave overnight so that the oil is infused with herb flavours. Do not refrigerate.

Drizzle the herb oil evenly over the pizza base.

Put the pizza straight onto the pavers in the preheated wood-fired oven using the paddle.

Allow to cook for 10 minutes, rotating occasionally until the base is golden brown.

Cut and serve.

NAPOLITANA

1 pizza base
8 fl oz (1 cup/250 ml) Napolitana sauce (see recipe p. 53)
1 lb (2 cups/450 g) mozzarella cheese
5 tablespoons anchovies

Spread Napolitana sauce evenly over the pizza base then top with mozzarella cheese and anchovies.

Put the pizza straight onto the pavers in the preheated wood-fired oven using the paddle.

Allow to cook for 10 minutes, rotating occasionally until the base is golden brown and the cheese has melted.

Cut and serve.

NOTE: Use Camembert cheese for a different taste but don't allow the cheese to melt too much or brown.

CARAMELIZED ONION

1 pizza base
4 fl oz (½ cup/125 ml) olive oil, plus extra for drizzling
4¼ lb (6 cups/1.9 kg) Spanish (Bermuda) onion, thinly sliced
6 garlic cloves
5 sprigs fresh thyme, leaves stripped from the stems
1 bay leaf
2½ oz (1 cup/75 g) mushrooms, sliced
8 oz (1 cup/225 g) goats' cheese
salt and pepper

MAKES 1 PIZZA

Put the olive oil, onions, garlic, thyme and bay leaf in a terracotta bowl. Push the bowl into a corner of the preheated wood-fired oven and stir occasionally until the oil has evaporated and the onions are soft. Remove the bay leaf.

Cover the pizza base with the onion mix and the sliced mushrooms then drizzle with some more olive oil.

Put the pizza straight onto the pavers in the preheated wood-fired oven using the paddle.

Allow to cook for 10–15 minutes, rotating occasionally, until the base is golden brown.

Crumble with goats' cheese. Cut and serve.

NOTE: Drizzle with balsamic glaze to give a zingy taste, if you like.

VEGETARIAN CALZONI

1 pizza base
¾ oz (¼ cup/20 g) eggplant
  (aubergine), sliced
1½ oz (¼ cup/45 g) zucchini
  (courgette), sliced
1¼ oz (¼ cup/40 g) capsicum (bell
  pepper), sliced
olive oil, for drizzling
salt and pepper

4 fl oz (½ cup/125 ml) Napolitana
  sauce (see recipe p. 53)
8 oz (1 cup/225 g) mozzarella cheese
1 oz (¼ cup/30 g) artichoke hearts,
  quartered

MAKES 1 PIZZA

Put the sliced eggplant, zucchini and capsicum in a baking tray. Sprinkle with oil and season with salt and pepper then place the tray in the preheated wood-fired oven for 15 minutes, or until soft.

Spread Napolitana sauce evenly over half of the base. Arrange the vegetables over the sauce and top with mozzarella. Fold uncoated pizza half over vegetables and cheese then crimp around edge with finger.

Put the pizza straight onto pavers in the preheated wood-fired oven using the paddle.

Allow to cook for 10 minutes, rotating occasionally, until the base and top are golden brown

Cut and serve.

POTATO & ROSEMARY

1 pizza base
4 fl oz (½ cup/125 ml) olive oil
8 oz (1 cups/225 g) mozzarella
  cheese
1 lb 2 oz (500 g) potato, boiled and
  sliced
10 oz (1 cup/275 g) Spanish
  (Bermuda) onion, diced
2 tablespoons dried rosemary

MAKES 1 PIZZA

Roll out your pizza base with rolling pin or by hand to a nice, round 30 cm circle.

Drizzle the pizza base with olive oil then arrange the sliced potato, onions and rosemary on top. Scatter over the mozzarella cheese.

Put the pizza straight onto pavers in the preheated wood-fired oven using the paddle.

Allow to cook for 10 minutes, rotating occasionally until the base is golden brown and the cheese has melted.

Cut and serve.

PRIMAVERA

1 pizza base
1½ oz (½ cup/45 g) eggplant
  (aubergine), sliced
3 oz (½ cup/85 g) zucchini
  (courgette), sliced
olive oil, to drizzle
salt and pepper
8 fl oz (1 cup/250 ml) Napolitana
  sauce (see recipe p. 53)
3 oz (½ cup/85 g) sun-dried

tomatoes, sliced
2½ oz (½ cup/75 g) yellow capsicum
  (bell pepper), sliced
1 lb (2 cups/450 g) mozzarella cheese

MAKES 1 PIZZA

Place sliced eggplant, zucchini and yellow pepper on a baking tray. Drizzle with oil and season well, then place the tray in the preheated wood-fired oven for 15 minutes, or until soft.

Spread Napolitana sauce evenly over the pizza base. Arrange the vegetables over the sauce and top with mozzarella.

Put the pizza straight onto pavers in the preheated wood-fired oven using the paddle.

Allow to cook for 10 minutes, rotating occasionally until the base is golden brown and the cheese has melted.

Cut and serve.

NOTE: Replace the vegetables with other favourites, if you like.

PUMPKIN PESTO

1 pizza base (see recipe p. 60)
1 lb (2 cups/450 g) butternut
  squash, chopped into ⅜ in (1 cm)
  dice dice
olive oil, for drizzling
8 fl oz (1 cup/250 ml) pesto sauce

1 lb (2 cups/450 g) feta cheese, diced
1 cup caramelized onion (see
  Caramelized Onion Pizza recipe on
  page 92)

Place the diced butternut squash on a baking tray. Drizzle with olive oil, then bake in the wood-fired oven for 10 minutes, or until soft.

Spread pesto sauce evenly over the pizza base. Scatter the cooked squash on top with the caramelized onion.

Put the pizza straight onto pavers in the preheated wood-fired oven using the paddle.

Allow to cook for 10 minutes, rotating occasionally, until the base is golden brown.

Arrange the diced feta on top. Cut and serve.

NOTE: Use sweet-potato instead of squash, if you like.

BARBEQUE CHICKEN CALZONI

1 pizza base
1 lb 2 oz (500 g) chicken breast
4 fl oz (½ cup/125 ml) Napolitana
  sauce (see recipe p. 53)
2½ oz (¼ cup/75 g) onion, diced
2½ oz (1 cup/75 g) mushrooms,
  sliced

2½ oz (1 cup/ 75 g) baby spinach
8 oz (1 cup/225 g) mozzarella cheese,
  shredded

Place the chicken on a baking tray and bake in wood-fired oven for 15 minutes, or until cooked through. When cool enough to handle, slice the chicken thinly.

Spread Napolitana sauce evenly over half the base. Arrange the chicken, onions, mushrooms and baby spinach over the sauce. Top with mozzarella.

Fold the uncoated pizza half over the chicken, vegetables and cheese, and crimp around the edge with your fingers.

Put straight onto the pavers in the preheated wood-fired oven using the pizza paddle.

Cook for 10 minutes, rotating occasionally, until the base and top are golden brown.

Cut and serve.

BARBEQUE CHICKEN

1 pizza base
8 fl oz (1 cup/250 ml) barbeque
  sauce (see recipe p. 64)
5 oz (1 cup/150 g) cooked chicken
  breast, diced
2½ oz (½ cup/75 g) red capsicum
  (bell pepper), diced
2½ oz (½ cup/75 g) green capsicum
  (bell pepper), diced

5 oz (½ cup/150 g) Spanish
  (Bermuda) onion, diced
1 lb (2 cups/450 g) mozzarella
  cheese
salt and peppers

Spread the barbeque sauce over the pizza base.

Scatter the chicken, pepper bells and onions on top, then scatter the mozzarella cheese over. season with salt and pepper.

Put the pizza straight onto pavers in the preheated wood-fired oven using the paddle.

Cook for 10–15 minutes, rotating occasionally, until the base is golden brown and the cheese is melted.

Cut and serve.

NOTE: Try smoked chicken, it's just as nice

SATAY CHICKEN

MAKES 1 PIZZA

1 pizza base
500 g (1 lb 2 oz) chicken breast
   marinated in satay sauce (see
   recipe p. 64)
4 fl oz (½ cup/125 ml) olive oil
1 lb (2 cups/450 g) mozzarella cheese
4 oz (½ cup/115 g) peanuts, crushed

Place the marinated chicken in the preheated wood-fired oven for 15 minutes until cooked through. Remove from the oven and allow to cook. Slice the meat.

Drizzle olive oil evenly over the pizza base, then arrange the sliced chicken on top. Scatter mozzarella cheese on top.

Put the pizza straight onto pavers in the preheated wood-fired oven using the paddle.

Allow to cook for 10 minutes, rotating occasionally, until the base is golden brown and the cheese has melted.

Sprinkle with crushed peanuts. Cut and serve.

PERI PERI CHICKEN

1 pizza base
1 lb 2 oz (500 g) chicken breast
    marinated in peri peri sauce (see
    recipe p. 66)
8 fl oz (1 cup/250 ml) Napolitana
    sauce (see recipe p. 53)
1 lb (2 cups/450 g) mozzarella cheese
5 oz (½ cup/150 g) red onion, diced

MAKES 1 PIZZA

Put the marinated chicken in a baking tray and bake in the preheated wood-fired oven for 15 minutes. Remove, allow to cool and slice.

Spread Napolitana sauce evenly over the pizza base then arrange the sliced chicken on top with the onion. Top with mozzarella cheese.

Put the pizza straight onto pavers in the preheated wood-fired oven using the paddle.

Allow to cook for 10 minutes, rotating occasionally until the base is golden brown and the cheese has melted.

Cut and serve.

TANDOORI CHICKEN

1 pizza base
1 lb 2 oz (500 g) chicken breast
  marinated in tandoori paste (see
  recipe p. 66)
8 fl oz (1 cup/250 ml) Napolitana
  sauce (see recipe p. 53)
1 lb (2 cups/450 g) mozzarella cheese
2½ oz (½ cup/75 g) capsicum (bell
  pepper), sliced

4 fl z (½ cup/125 ml) Greek (strained
  plain) yogurt

MAKES 1 PIZZA

Place the marinated chicken in a baking tray and place in the preheated wood-fired oven for 15 minutes. Remove the chicken, allow to cool and slice the meat.

Spread Napolitana sauce evenly over the pizza base. Arrange the sliced chicken on top with the capsicum, then top with mozzarella cheese.

Put the pizza straight onto pavers in the preheated wood-fired oven using the paddle.

Allow to cook for 10 minutes, rotating occasionally, until the base is golden brown and the cheese has melted.

Drizzle with yogurt. Cut and serve.

BACON & EGG

1 pizza base
8 fl oz (1 cup/250 ml) barbeque
  sauce (see recipe p. 64)
6 oz (1 cup/175 g) bacon, diced
1 lb (2 cups/450 g) mozzarella cheese
4 eggs

MAKES 1 PIZZA

Spread Barbeque sauce evenly over the pizza base. Arrange the diced bacon around the pizza and top with mozzarella cheese.

Put straight onto the pavers in the preheated wood-fired oven using a paddle.

Cook for 5 minutes rotating occasionally. Remove from the oven and crack the eggs on top. Return to the oven for another 5 minutes, rotating occasionally, until the base is golden brown, the cheese has melted and the eggs are cooked.

Cut and serve.

NOTE: For a late brunch, roll out pizza bases to 4 in (10 cm) diameter and top each with 1 egg.

TROPICAL

1 pizza base
8 fl oz (1 cup/250 ml) Napolitana
  sauce (see recipe p. 53)
6 oz (1 cup/175 g) ham, diced
6 oz (1 cup/175 g) pineapple, diced
1 lb (2 cups/450 g) mozzarella cheese

MAKES 1 PIZZA

Spread Napolitana sauce evenly over the pizza base. Scatter diced ham and pineapple over the surface. Top with mozzarella cheese.

Put the pizza straight onto pavers in the preheated wood-fired oven using the paddle.

Allow to cook for 10 minutes, rotating occasionally, until the base is golden brown and the cheese has melted.

Cut and serve.

FOUR SEASONS

1 pizza base
8 fl oz (1 cup/250 ml) Napolitana
   sauce (see recipe p. 53)
6 oz (1 cup/175 g) ham, sliced
2½ oz (1 cup/75 g) mushrooms,
   sliced
3 oz (1 cup/85 g) artichoke, quarters
3 oz (½ cup/85 g) Kalamata olives

1 lb (2 cups/450 g) mozzarella cheese

MAKES 1 PIZZA

Roll out your pizza base with rolling pin or by hand to a nice, round 30cm circle.

Spread Napolitana sauce evenly over the pizza base. Arrange the ham, mushrooms, artichoke quarters and olives over the surface then top with mozzarella cheese.

Put the pizza straight onto the pavers in the preheated wood-fired oven using the paddle.

Cook for 10 minutes, rotating occasionally, until the base is golden brown and the cheese has melted.

Cut and serve.

NOTE: This pizza is also great with a Barbeque sauce base.

PESTO & PROSCIUTTO

MAKES 1 PIZZA

1 pizza base
8 fl oz (1 cup/250 ml) pesto sauce
   (see recipe p. 60)
7 oz (200 g) prosciutto, sliced
4 oz (½ cup/115 g) sun-dried
   tomatoes
12 oz (1½ cups/375 g) bocconcini
   cheese, sliced

Spread the pesto sauce evenly over the pizza base. Arrange the sliced prosciutto and sun-dried tomatoes on top, then arrange bocconcini cheese on top.

Put the pizza straight onto pavers in the preheated wood-fired oven using the paddle.

Allow to cook for 10 minutes, rotating occasionally, until the base is golden brown and the cheese has melted.

Cut and serve.

HOT CHORIZO

1 pizza base
8 fl oz (1 cup/250 ml) Napolitana
sauce (see recipe p. 53)
8 oz (2 cups/225 g) hot chorizo,
sliced
5 oz (½ cup/150 g) onion, diced
2½ oz (½ cup/75 g) capsicum (bell
pepper), diced
1 lb (2 cups/450 g) mozzarella cheese

Spread Napolitana sauce evenly over the pizza base, then arrange the chorizo, onion and capsicum on the pizza and top with mozzarella cheese.

Put the pizza straight onto the pavers in the preheated wood-fired oven using the paddle.

Allow to cook for 10 minutes, rotating occasionally, until the base is golden brown and the cheese has melted.

Cut and serve.

NOTE: Use mild chorizo if you prefer, or add fresh chilli for a hotter pizza taste.

MEAT LOVERS

1 pizza base
8 fl oz (1 cup/250 ml) barbeque
*   sauce (see recipe p. 64)*
6 oz (1 cup/175 g) ham, diced
4 oz (1 cup/115 g) pepperoni, sliced
6 oz (1 cup/175 g) bacon, diced
4 oz (1 cup/115 g) chorizo, sliced
1 lb (2 cups/450 g) mozzarella cheese

Spread Barbeque sauce evenly over the pizza base. Arrange diced ham, sliced pepperoni, diced bacon and sliced chorizo around the pizza top with the mozzarella cheese.

Put the pizza straight onto the pavers in the preheated wood-fired oven using the paddle.

Allow to cook for 10 minutes, rotating occasionally, until the base is golden brown and the cheese has melted.

Cut and serve.

NOTE: For an 'inferno' or meat lover's pizza, replace Napolitana sauce with spicy sauce and hot chorizo!

PEPPERONI

1 pizza base
8 fl oz (1 cup/250 ml) Napolitana sauce (see recipe p. 53)
6 oz (1 cup/175 g) pepperoni
1 lb (2 cups/450 g) mozzarella cheese
salt and pepper

MAKES 1 PIZZA

Spread the Napolitana sauce evenly on the pizza base.

Cover ywith pepperoni and sprinkle with mozzarella cheese. Season to taste.

Put the pizza straight onto the pavers in the preheated wood-fired oven using the paddle.

Allow to cook for 10 minutes, rotating occasionally, until the base is golden brown and the cheese has melted.

Cut and serve.

PORK & FENNEL

1 pizza base
4 fl oz (½ cup/125 ml) olive oil
1 lb (2 cups/450 g) minced (ground)
   pork
2 fresh fennel, sliced
8 oz (1 cup/225 g) goats' cheese
¼ bunch dill, chopped

MAKES 1 PIZZA

Place pork mince on a tray. Lightly drizzle with oil and place into your wood-fired oven. Cook for 10 minutes. Remove, then allow to cool. Crumble into small pieces.

Drizzle olive oil evenly over the pizza base. Arrange the cooked pork mince and sliced fennel on top.

Put the pizza straight onto pavers in the preheated wood-fired oven using the paddle.

Allow to cook for 10 minutes, rotating occasionally until the base is golden brown.

Crumble over the goats' cheese and dill.

Cut and serve.

PEPPERONI CALZONI

1 pizza base
4 fl oz (½ cup/125 ml) Napolitana
  sauce (see recipe p. 53)
6 oz (1 cup/175 g) pepperoni, sliced
1½ oz (¼ cup/40 g) kalamata olives
8 oz (1 cup/225 g) mozzarella cheese

MAKES 1 PIZZA

Spread Napolitana sauce evenly over half of the base. Arrange the pepperoni and olives on top and cover with mozzarella.

Fold over the other half of the dough circle, and crimp around edge with your fingers.

Put the pizza straight onto pavers in the preheated wood-fired oven using the paddle.

Allow to cook for 10 minutes, rotating occasionally until the base and top are golden brown.

Cut and serve.

PANCETTA & MUSHROOM

1 pizza base
8 fl oz (1 cup/250 ml) Napolitana
   sauce (see recipe p. 53)
6 marinated artichokes or artichoke
   hearts, quartered
7 oz (200 g) pancetta, sliced
5 oz (½ cup/150 g) spring onion,
   finely chopped

2½ oz (1 cup/75 g) mushrooms,
   sliced
1 lb (2 cups/450 g) mozzarella cheese

Spread Napolitana sauce evenly over the pizza base. Arrange the artichoke, sliced pancetta, chopped onion and sliced mushroom on top, then scatter over the mozzarella cheese.

Put the pizza straight onto the pavers in the preheated wood-fired oven using the paddle.

Allow to cook for 10 minutes, rotating occasionally, until the base is golden brown and the cheese has melted.

Cut and serve.

SUPREME

1 pizza base
8 fl oz (1 cup/250 ml) Napolitana
  sauce (see recipe p. 53)
3 oz (½ cup/85 g) ham, diced
1½ oz (½ cup/45 g) mushrooms,
  sliced
2 oz (½ cup/60 g) salami, sliced
5 oz (½ cup/150 g) onion, diced
2½ oz (½ cup/75 g) capsicum (bell
  pepper), diced

3 oz (½ cup/85 g) pineapple, diced
1½ oz (¼ cup/40 g) kalamata olives
1 lb (2 cups/450 g) mozzarella cheese

MAKES 1 PIZZA

Spread Napolitana sauce evenly over the pizza base. Arrange diced ham, sliced mushrooms, sliced salami, diced onion, capsicum, pineapple and olives on top. Evenly scatter with mozzarella cheese.

Put the pizza straight onto pavers in the preheated wood-fired oven using the paddle.

Allow to cook for 10 minutes, rotating occasionally, until the base is golden brown and the cheese has melted.

Cut and serve.

PROSCIUTTO

1 pizza base
8 fl oz (1 cup/250 ml) Napolitana
   sauce (see recipe p. 53)
10 slices prosciutto
2½ oz (½ cup/75 g) capsicum (bell
   pepper), sliced
1 lb (2 cups/450 g) bocconcini cheese,
   sliced
10 fresh basil leaves, torn

MAKES 1 PIZZA

Spread Napolitana sauce evenly over the pizza base. Arrange the prosciutto and sliced capsicum around the pizza, then top with sliced Bocconcini cheese.

Put the pizza straight onto the pavers in the preheated wood-fired oven using the paddle.

Allow to cook for 10 minutes, rotating occasionally, until the base is golden brown and the cheese has melted.

Sprinkle with basil. Cut and serve.

BOLOGNESE

1 pizza base
12 fl oz (1½ cups/350 g) Bolognese
   sauce (see recipe p. 59)
1 lb (450 g/2 cups) mozzarella cheese

MAKES 1 PIZZA

Spread Bolognese sauce evenly over the pizza base, then top with mozzarella cheese.

Put the pizza straight onto pavers in the preheated wood-fired oven using the paddle.

Cook for 10 minutes, rotating occasionally, until the base is golden brown and the cheese has melted.

Cut and serve.

NACHO

1 pizza base
8 fl oz (1 cup/250 ml) barbeque sauce (see recipe p. 64)
12 oz (1½ cups/350 g) Cheddar (tasty) cheese
2 cups nacho mince (ground beef)
(3½ oz (100 g)
4 fl oz (½ cup/125 ml) sour cream
½ cup guacamole (see recipe p. 67)
2 cups corn chips
4 fl oz (½ cup/125 ml) salsa sauce (see recipe p. 67)

NACHO MINCE (GROUND BEEF)
Bolognese sauce (see recipe p. 59)
1 tbsp chilli powder
1 tbsp smoked paprika
1 tbsp Taco seasoning

Mix all spices into your Bolognese sauce.

Spread Nacho mince evenly over base, top with tasty cheese.

Put the pizza straight onto the pavers in the preheated wood-fired oven using the paddle.

Allow to cook for 10 minutes, rotating using your pizza spatula until base is golden brown and cheese has melted.

Cut then in centre of pizza put corn chips topped with sour cream, guacamole, salsa sauce and serve.

NOTE: Use Bolognese sauce just mix a packet of nacho seasoning also add mixed beans

MOROCCAN LAMB

1 pizza base
2 lamb back-strap (loin), marinated
  with Moroccan spices
4 fl oz (½ cup/125 ml) olive oil
 oz (1 cup/175 g) Spanish (Bermuda)
  onion, diced
2 tablespoons dried rosemary
8 oz (1 cup/225 g) feta cheese
8 fl oz (1 cup/250 ml) Greek

(strained plain) yogurt
64 tablespoons Moroccan spices
mint leaves, to garnish

MAKES 1 PIZZA

Place the marinated Moroccan lamb on a baking tray. Bake for 15 minutes then slice thinly.

Drizzle olive oil evenly over the pizza base, then spread lamb, onions and rosemary on top.

Put the pizza straight onto the pavers in the preheated wood-fired oven using the paddle.

Allow to cook for 10 minutes, rotating occasionally, until the base is golden brown.

Crumble feta cheese over the top, drizzle with yogurt and garnish with mint leaves

Cut and serve.

SHRIMP

1 pizza base
8 fl oz (1 cup/250 ml) Napolitana
   sauce (see recipe p. 53)
3 oz (½ cup/85 g) zucchini
   (courgette), sliced
1 lb 2 oz (500 g) peeled shrimp
   (prawns)
7 oz (200 g) cherry tomatoes
1 teaspoon chilli flakes

1 lb (2 cups/450 g) mozzarella cheese
2½ oz (1 cup/75 g) rocket (arugula)

MAKES 1 PIZZA

Spread Napolitana sauce evenly over the pizza base. Arrange the sliced zucchini, shrimps and cherry tomatoes on top then sprinkle with chilli top with mozzarella cheese.

Put the pizza straight onto pavers in the preheated wood-fired oven using the paddle.

Allow to cook for 10 minutes, rotating occasionally using your pizza spatula until base is golden brown and cheese has melted.

Place the rocket on top, cut and serve.

NOTE: Add any seafood you like, such as calamari, mussels, salmon or octopus.

SMOKED SALMON

1 pizza base
4 fl oz (½ cup/125 ml) olive oil
1 lb 2 oz (500 g) smoked salmon,
  sliced
8 oz (1 cup/225 g) cherry tomatoes,
  halved
1 avocado, sliced
1¾ oz (50 g) baby capers
1 lb (2 cups/450 g) mozzarella cheese

juice of 1 lemon

MAKES 1 PIZZA

Drizzle the pizza base with olive oil , then arrange the smoked salmon on the surface. Add the cherry tomato halves, sliced avocado and capers. Top with mozzarella cheese

Put the pizza straight onto pavers in the preheated wood-fired oven using the paddle.

Allow to cook for 10 minutes, rotating occasionally, until the base is golden brown.

Cut and serve with some freshly squeezed lemon.

BLT

1 basic pizza dough
1 cup barbeque sauce
2 cup Mozzarella cheese
1 cup bacon, diced
2 tomatoes, sliced
1 cup shredded lettuce

MAKES 1 PIZZA

Roll out your pizza base with rolling pin or by hand to a nice, round 30cm circle.

Spread barbeque sauce evenly over base, place diced bacon, sliced tomato around pizza top with mozzarella cheese.

Put straight onto pavers in your preheated wood-fired oven

Allow to cook for 10 minutes, rotating occasionally using your pizza spatula until the base is golden brown and the cheese has melted.

Sprinkle with shredded lettuce. Cut and serve.

NUTELLA

1 pizza base
1 lb 6 oz (2 cups/600 g) Nutella
3½ oz (100 g) strawberries, halved
1 lb 2 oz (500 g) mascarpone

Put the pizza straight onto the pavers in the preheated wood-fired oven using the paddle.

Allow to bake for 5 minutes then remove from the oven. Spread Nutella evenly on top, then return to the oven.

Bake for 5 minutes, rotating occasionally until the base is golden brown.

Arrange the strawberries on top, then serve with a dollop of mascarpone.

NOTE: Replace the mascarpone with ice cream or whipped cream, if you like.

PEAR & GORGONZOLA

1 pizza base
2 fl oz (¼ cup/60 ml) olive oil
5 oz (150 g) provolone cheese, sliced
2 pears, peeled and sliced
2 oz (60 g) walnuts, crushed
3½ oz (100 g) gorgonzola cheese

MAKES 1 PIZZA

Drizzle olive oil evenly over the pizza base. Arrange the sliced provolone cheese and sliced pear on top. Scatter the walnut evenly over the surface then top with crumbled gorgonzola.

Put the pizza straight onto pavers in the preheated wood-fired oven using the paddle.

Allow to bake for 10 minutes, rotating occasionally until the base is golden brown and the cheese has melted.

Cut and serve.

NOTE: Replace pears with apples or other stone fruits, if you like. Dust the top with sugar and bake until it caramelises.

ROAST & BAKE

HOMEMADE BREAD

1 oz (35 g) fresh yeast
13 fl oz (440 ml) warm water
3 lb 5 oz (1.6 kg) strong white bread
  flour, plus extra for dusting
1⅓ oz (10 g) salt
1 fl oz (25 ml) olive oil

Mix the yeast with the warm water in a large bowl. Leave for 10 minutes until the yeast dissolves and the liquid becomes creamy.

Sift the flour into a large bowl and make a well in the centre. Pour in the yeast mixture and the salt. Mix well then slowly add the olive oil.

When the dough comes together, turn out onto a lightly floured surface and knead until smooth and elastic.

Lightly rub the dough ball with oil, return it to the bowl, cover with a damp cloth and set aside in a warm place until doubled in volume, about 45 minutes.

Tip the dough out onto a lightly floured surface and knead lightly. Divide into 3 equal rounds and set aside to rest for another 5 minutes.

Bake on the pavers in the preheated wood-fired oven for 45 minutes, or until the base and top are golden brown.

BUFFALO CHICKEN DRUMSTICKS

4½ lb (2 kg) chicken thighs

MARINADE
8 fl oz (1 cup/250 ml) barbeque
   sauce (see recipe p. 64)
2 fl oz (¼ cup/60 ml) Worcestershire
   sauce
2 tablespoons balsamic vinegar

2 tablespoons sweet paprika
2 tablespoons cayenne pepper
salt
oil, for greasing

SERVES 5 PEOPLE.

To make the marinade, in a large glass or ceramic bowl, mix the Barbeque sauce, Worcestershire sauce, balsamic vinegar, sweet paprika, cayenne pepper and salt together.

Place the chicken in the marinade and leave overnight to absorb all the flavours.

The following morning, place the chicken on a greased baking sheet and cover with foil.

Place the excess marinade in a terracotta pot in the corner of the wood-fired oven to reduce.

Add the baking sheet with the chicken wings and leave to cook for 20 minutes. Remove the foil and continue to cook for 10 minutes until crispy and golden brown.

Drizzle with reduced marinade just before serving.

OVEN ROASTED BEEF RIBS

8¾ lbs (4 kg) beef ribs
4 fl oz (½ cup/125 ml) Dijon
 mustard
3 garlic cloves, crushed
salt and pepper 2 sprigs fresh
 rosemary

SERVES 5 PEOPLE.

Rub the ribs with Dijon mustard, garlic and seasoning. Refrigerate overnight in a glass or ceramic dish to marinate.

The following morning, place on an oiled tray, scatter fresh rosemary on top, cover with kitchen foil and place into the preheated wood-fired oven.

Cook for 50 minutes then remove the foil.

Continue to cook until golden brown and the meat is almost starting to fall off the bone, about 35 minutes.

Remove from the oven and cut into single or double pieces.

Serve with your roasted vegetables (see recipe p. 170).

NOTE: Replace the beef ribs with pork or rack of lamb. The cooking times are similar. Alternatively, marinate the beef ribs with Barbeque sauce (see recipe p. 64).

OVEN ROAST

6¾ lb (3 kg) either lamb leg, boned,
   or pork neck or beef rump or whole
   chicken
3 sprigs rosemary
3 garlic cloves, quartered
4 fl oz (½ cup/125 ml) olive oil
salt and pepper

SERVES 5 PEOPLE

Slash the meat with a sharp knife and push the garlic and rosemary in the slashes. Rub all over with olive oil. Season well and place in a baking tray. Cover with kitchen foil.

Place the meat in the preheated wood-fired oven for 45 minutes. Remove the foil and leave for another 30 minutes until the skin begins to crisp.

Serve with roasted vegetables.

COOKING TIMES:
    Lamb: 30 minutes per kg
    Beef: 25 minutes for rare; 35 minutes for medium; and 45 minutes for well done, per kg
    Pork: 30 minutes per kg
    Chicken: 20 minutes per kg

HONEY SAGE SALMON

2 salmon fillets, each 12 oz (350 g)
   skin on
salt and pepper
2 tablespoons dried sage
3 oz (85 g) butter
6 tablespoons honey

SERVES 2 PEOPLE.

Rub the seasoning and sage onto the flesh side of the salmon.

Put the butter in a terracotta pot or ovenproof pan and brown in the preheated wood-fired oven.

Take the dish out then place the salmon, flesh-side down, into the butter and return the container to the oven for 5 minutes.

Remove from the oven, turn the fish over and pour the honey on the salmon. Return to the oven for 10–15 minutes until the skin crisps ups.

Serve with a garden salad or roasted vegetables.

ROASTED VEGETABLES

6 potatoes, large peeled
2 sweet potatoes, peeled
3 carrots, large peeled
1 butternut pumpkin (squash), peeled
½ cup olive oil
seasoning

SERVES 5 PEOPLE

Cut all your vegetables to the same size.

Season and rub with oil. Place on a tray and cover with foil.

Place into your pre-heated wood fire oven for 25 minutes.

Remove foil and leave for a further 15 minutes until vegetable are soft .

Take out and serve with your lamb roast, honey sage salmon or roast beef ribs.

First published in 2014 by New Holland Publishers
This edition published in 2019 by New Holland Publishers
Sydney

Level 1, 178 Fox Valley Road, Wahroonga, NSW 2076, Australia

newhollandpublishers.com

A record of this book is held at the National Library of Australia.

ISBN 9781760791209

Managing Director: Fiona Schultz
Publisher: Alan Whiticker
Editor: Simona Hill
Designer: Lorena Susak
Photographs: Joe Filshie
Production Director: Arlene Gippert
Printed in China

10 9 8 7 6 5 4 3 2

Keep up with New Holland Publishers:

 NewHollandPublishers
 @newhollandpublishers